Fragrance of Freedom

Discovering Peace through Mothering

Written by Heena Vasani, illustrated by her children,
Jamie and Sienna Chahal

Matador
Unit E2, Airfield Business Park
Harrison Road
Market Harborough
LE16 7UL
Email: books@troubador.co.uk
Web: www.troubador.co.uk/matador
Twitter: @matadorbooks
www.heenavasani.com

ISBN 978 1788039 420

British Library Cataloguing in Publication Data.
A catalogue record for this book is available from the British Library.

Printed and bound in the UK by TJ Books Limited, Padstow, Cornwall
Typeset in 11pt Adobe Garamond Pro by Troubador Publishing Ltd, Leicester, UK

Matador is an imprint of Troubador Publishing Ltd

"An extraordinary book for parents and guardians of the future. A book filled with humanity's most essential values, spiritual longing and belonging, through the lives of our future eyes, ears, and hearts – those of our children.

This book will bring calm, beauty, innocence, healing, remembrance, and transparency into people's lives."

Chloë Goodchild

This book is dedicated to my inner child,
and to yours,
to my two inspiring children,
Jamie and Sienna,
to my four wonderful nieces,
Shiana, Nicole, Simran, and Summer,
and to all the delightful children of the world.

Contents

Acknowledgements

This book is a soul conversation between myself and my two children. It is a dialogue of their water colour paintings and what that pure language of colour, light, space, natural imagery and beauty opened and revealed within me – glimpses of our True Nature, our shared Being. It is an invitation to remember a Truth beyond the intellect.

I am enormously grateful to my beloved, paternal grandmother, an elder, who has been a constant and abiding Presence in my life.

However, this book is also a gift from my mother, a spiritual teacher, who left my world when I was a young child only to return for just a short while, some twenty years later, when I was with child myself.

In addition, I would like to thank my cherished family and friends for the support and love they have shared in helping me to bring this message into the world.

I would also like to express my sincere appreciation to my kidney transplant surgeon Dr Ossie Fernando, at the Royal Free Hospital, London, for performing my life saving operation in 1997, and to my attentive nurse Catherine O'Malley, for nursing me back to strength. Love and warmth to Manny Chahal, my partner at the time, for his dedicated support and companionship throughout. The healthy kidney continues to live on in my body today.

Loving thanks to my dear friends and teachers who along the path have deeply touched my heart, inspired me with their wisdom and radiant teachings, and have helped shape my life and this book: Catherine Walsh, Ruth Geiger, Maggie Rodriguez, Sheena Vasani, Dawn Golten, Laura Benning, Ellie Tasevska, Jeff and Sue Allen, Pam Carruthers, Sandy Levey-Lundén, Len Satov, Miranda Macpherson, Chloe Goodchild, Eckhart Tolle, Rupert Spira, Ian Patrick and the Miracle Network, and (Chuck Spezzano and) the Psychology of Vision. Also to the teachings of Rumi, Kahlil Gibran and A Course in Miracles, all of which which lie within the pages of this book.

Profound gratitude to Nick Vane, Jamie's middle-school teacher, and to Inga and Miss Anna, Sienna's kindergarten teachers at the Waldorf Steiner School, Hertfordshire – for honouring and keeping the artistry within my children alive.

And finally, abundant blessings to my wonderful friend Oriana Howes who has lovingly and graciously helped edit this book, and to my wise guide Vladik, who kindly shared with me the teachings of Mooji and Papaji and taught me of the Tao as he travels the world, following his flow, as the flow.

Foreword

I am privileged to share and to celebrate Heena Vasani's unique journey and encounter with the sacred feminine in *Fragrance of Freedom*. Heena is the dedicated mother of Jamie and Sienna, whose presence also inspired her calling to become a spiritual mother and mentor to others. Heena is a dear friend, and treasured practitioner of *The Naked Voice* community. She has participated for many years in our retreats focusing on voice as a spiritual practice. And it has been there that I have been fortunate to witness Heena's encounter with the sacred feminine, her unique journey of awakening, and to discover its resonant echoes in my own personal experience as a mother and spiritual mentor.

Fragrance of Freedom celebrates Heena's remarkable East-West journey through childhood and the painful physical absence of her blood mother, into the living presence and wondrous joy of Unconditional Love. Here is a book whose utter simplicity, penetrating dialogue, and transparent enquiry into the nature of true motherhood returns us to the essence of Life itself. Heena Vasani's message is a wisdom call that honours both our inner child and the conscious core truths for compassionate mothering, at home, in our families, and the wider community.

Fragrance of Freedom is the magical revelation of one woman's self-determination to forgive, to heal, to overcome, and to transform the shadow and pain of an ancestral wound into the compassionate teachings for conscious parenthood. And it is Heena's direct experience as the mother of Jamie and Sienna that has so uniquely inspired the poetic style and visual content of her remarkable book. *Fragrance of Freedom* is the fruit of a unique journey transforming personal suffering into the flower of spiritual awareness.

Fragrance of Freedom is both a prayer and a mother's

call to action on behalf of children everywhere. Exquisitely designed, and illustrated by Heena's children, this book invites us to reflect deeply on the true conditions required for conscious parenting and the wellbeing of children entrusted to our care.

Reading **Fragrance of Freedom** is like being embraced by the Great Mother, Anandamayi, Sophia, Ma Gaia. And I have been deeply touched by Heena's humble capacity to demonstrate through her own life story how to undertake the essential rite of passage through suffering into wisdom eldership, so as to restore honour and wholeness to the essential theme of our time, *Unconditional Loving Presence*.

Heena has communicated through the intensity of her own graceful passage how to transform the illusions of separateness into an all-inclusive relationship with Life in all its forms, by Love's grace, and its significance for NOW.

And I have been deeply moved to remember once again

in Heena's autobiography – also included in this book – the several key initiation moments and rites of passage that Heena has patiently and courageously collaborated with, as in her attention to the healing with her stepmother, and to the passing of her own mother, and more recently her grandmother.

In **Fragrance of Freedom**, Heena Vasani demonstrates that by facing our suffering we unearth the koan, with its fierce gift which draws us home to the Source with sudden, unexpected speed, or, to turn our gaze once more, into the Infinite Light of Love's Presence.

Chloë Goodchild

Author, international singer, and founder of *The Naked Voice Foundation*

www.thenakedvoice.com

Preface

This has been a twenty-five-year inner journey, in which I have been guided to slowly let go of the busy, material world which no longer served me. It has enabled me to deepen and listen to the quiet, still voice of my heart so that I could, in turn, honour the calling of my children's souls; our collective Soul. Their demands were persistent and precise, and called me to repeatedly turn within, forgive and keep choosing Truth. In doing so, simplicity, clarity, and grace arose and were experienced in everyday life. There was no room for negotiation. Such is the nature of Truth.

My mother left when I was very young and, in doing so, she bequeathed a devastating life lesson, leaving me with a profound belief in separation. I carried tremendous pain and sadness throughout my childhood, as well as an internal echo that I was neither loved nor lovable. Traditional Indian roles, family expectations and strict rules both governed and silenced my young life. And so it was written that an inner journey was destined to be taken.

One night, in the depths of my despair, I silently cried out for help, and the universe purposefully answered me by placing two young children in my path. Now I was a mother, and there was nowhere to hide, for my heart knew only too well of their potential plight if I were to leave. So, one step at a time and with as much self-love as I could muster, I surrendered to this calling. There was no choice but to turn within and to listen intently, since wisdom always speaks through silence. Mothering therefore became my spiritual practice – my *sadhana* – my devotion, and it led to a peace and tranquillity not only within, but also externally. A Truth beyond the intellect had begun to reveal itself, and I found that beyond my childhood pain and cultural conditioning lay a gateway to a most precious gift.

Trust

At the top of a tower, my daughter and I were buckled into our harnesses, each attached to a zip wire. The instructor shouted one, two, three, and immediately Sienna jumped off, free falling into the sky and squealing with delight. I, on the other hand, just stood there in the damp clouds, momentarily frozen. The realisation dawned on me that I would have to take this journey alone.

I peered down. I couldn't see the ground and my mind told me, *I can't do this!* I watched Sienna, way off in the distance now. She had trusted the process, as always.

I contemplated climbing back down the staircase to the safety of the ground, but by now there were crowds of people in the stairwell.

My instructor told me I had already done the hard work – saying Yes in the first place, ascending the spiral tower with all its complexity, and withstanding the gusty wind that had tried hard to knock me off balance. However, now it was time to jump off, to have fun and enjoy the ride.

I recall likening it to my life and this book…

I took a deep breath… I thought, this is exactly where I am… just about to jump off into the unknown. Yet who was I to take up space in the world, use my voice, my creativity? I felt vulnerable. And standing there, I allowed myself to really, fully feel into my fear.

I took another deep breath.

The instructor couldn't have been nearer to the truth. Indeed, my whole journey had been one steep climb with two young children by my side, but now they were in their teens, and gaining confidence in their own intuition, mastery, and lives. I had simply outgrown my old life, yet was still clinging to it. There was no going back and this book, which was started almost three years ago, no longer belonged to me but to Life itself.

I looked down once more and the instructor reminded me to simply rest into the harness and feel its support.

Of course. It was clear now. I had forgotten that my inherent peace and safety resided quietly within, believing I was the fear, the mind, the voice of the ego.

I sank back into the harness and took off on my sky ride, resting in the arms of grace as my body fell, totally surrendered, knowing with every beat of my heart that I had never been alone. I stretched out my arms and basked in deep gratitude, as I smelt the sweet fragrance of my innate Freedom. When I reached the sandy beach and relayed my experience I was told that people with 'childhood trust issues' always find it difficult to jump. These words sum it up beautifully, yet I have moved beyond them. And this book comes to you simply because I was willing to keep feeling, opening, trusting and surrendering one baby step at a time…

This book is meditative in nature

This book is meditative in nature and gently guides you back into Stillness, the Loving Presence of awareness, the very essence of your Being. I invite you to really take your time reading it. Savour your experience. Pause and reflect, and in doing so, the Stillness which resides prior to the words themselves will be revealed.

The insights and paintings have arisen from the very same Stillness, and they hold the power to penetrate your heart. As you slowly turn the pages, you may find that your thoughts start to dissipate and you begin to become aware of a greater sense of aliveness, silence, and peace within.

Much like a flower, may the colours and the fragrance of this book offer you the scent of home, and open your exquisite heart.

The Message

Each of us longs to be healed of the wound which sits in the heart of humanity, the belief that we are a separated self, imprisoned within a body.

As human beings, living in this world of form and very identified with the conditioned, thinking mind, we have no real sense of our true essential nature, an inner peace, a Stillness which is free of limitations, whole and interconnected with all of life.

Yet our children, through their very birth, prompt in each one of us the potential of an awakening to that Presence.

They offer us the opportunity to be reminded, touched, humbled even, by the beauty and mystery of our extraordinary existence.

"*Fragrance of Freedom* is our innate, peaceful essence – the authentic scent of who we truly are. This intimate, yet infinite, essential Self reveals itself silently within us all, but is often overlooked, and recognised by only a few."

HEENA VASANI

Note: Throughout this book there is reference to the child as "she". This has been used simply for the purpose of simplicity and "he" or "they" could equally be substituted by the reader.

FRAGRANCE of FREEDOM

Discovering
Peace
through
Mothering...

by Heena Vasani

Illustrated by her two children Jamie and Sienna

Dear Child,

I believe the pain is lodged deep within me and my
    harmful thoughts run even deeper.
I love you dearly, yet my grief is extreme and my
    sadness so cumbersome.
I believe I was never cut out to be a mother.
I cannot bond with you and I cannot rest with you.
I know not how to love, and wish to spare you from
    my sickness.
I believe I am not able to love.
I believe I am not loved.
I believe I am not lovable.
I fear love and I believe I cannot mother you.
Please forgive me.

Your Mother.

At the deepest level of Truth…

10

Children are teachers of Unconditional Love.

Angels. Love Incarnate.

Each child a miraculous star,
lifting the consciousness of our homes.

Giving birth
to
a mother,
a father,
a family.

16

Divine Beings, here to open our hearts and free our minds.

Inviting us to awaken from the dream of separation
and from the suffering…

…the fear and the pain that seems to permeate our lives.

Our young child restores to us a world of
Love, Peace, Truth, Creativity,

Presence, Being, Home…

Doubt not this child's incarnation,
for it has been divinely planned.

In the realms beyond time, this soul set an intention
to bestow sanctity upon its chosen family.

She comes with one
burning question in her heart:

24

"Are
you ready
to be true to
yourself?"

For her mother and father
have been asleep to the

Love

that resides within them.

They have forgotten how to be in Life's flow, and to connect with the heart of all living things…

Setting sail from the world of Spirit, this child carries a blueprint to highlight and harmonise our inner terrains.

And she carries the wisdom of miracles and mysticism, which will transform the way we perceive our world, our families, and each other.

Give her not your sight,

but instead, let her reveal her own vision.

Welcome

this

darling

soul…

…who has answered your silent cry for help and humanity's call for Love.

She
comes
bearing
gifts.

Simplicity,
Clarity,
and Grace.

Honour her Presence,
delicate yet strong.

And hold her in a deep, warm space of Love
so she may slowly emerge, as nature intends…

Water her, but mould her not.

For you know not her purpose here on Earth.

Listen to the magnificence
of her song.

What colour is it today?

Encourage her to truly feel, so she may go beyond her feelings, remaining rooted in her wisdom and her Truth.

For her safety lies within.

Encourage her to cultivate pure intuition, so her dance may bring joy and unity to a world of disharmony…

Let your heart be
nourished by her

Unconditional Love:

Her simple, bright light.
Her authentic voice.
Her unique vibration.

She is intelligent. Pay attention to her.
She is wise. Take heed.
And like the sun,
she shines
eternally.

For it seems humanity is asleep to a deeper Truth…

Reconnect to this beloved child's birth, to the moment she first greeted you.

Your eyes met and your hearts were connected, held in a timeless space of deep Love, wisdom, and beauty.

Resting in and as this Stillness, you felt alive, and awake.

This still, silent awareness exists behind the thinking mind and the five senses.
It is your true nature,
your true essence.

It is here where the divine within the mother recognises and meets the divine within the child.
As One Love.
As One Self.
As One Being.

It is the divine which invites you to mother effortlessly, from this Stillness.

For she has already called you to slow down,

reminding you of the simplicity of life,

reconnecting you to the silence and beauty of nature,

taking you back into the Stillness within.

Move beyond your thoughts and feelings,
and become **aware** of this Stillness.

Gently begin to sense yourself as this awareness,
this Loving Presence, which shines in all hearts as One Love.

This is her gift to you.

Be open to receive.

42

Begin to feel the gentle rhythm of your heart once more.

And allow the Soul of Mother Earth to nourish the mother within you.

Rest here and be still, for there is only One heartbeat and One Divine Mother.

44

She heralds compassionate communication, humility and peace and invites you to open every doorway to your heart, your innermost sanctuary, so that community, unity and Oneness may abide.

For Mother Earth has wished it so…

Every child is a
creator, aligned with
her divinity, her pure
intuition, her joy.

In touch with her essence, her true Self.

At One with pure consciousness, she is limitless, boundless.

Do you remember this place?

The sense of being truly at Home, carefree in your artistry? Your mastery?

Watch with tenderness and love as she creates.

She asks you to mother naturally from this Stillness.

As parents, we have been asleep to the yearning of our souls, to the quiet voice within, and to her request – that we parent with Presence.

Trapped in the stories of our ancestors and our families, where wounds, disagreements and unspoken words now fill our minds, we can no longer hear our calling.

We can no longer feel the connection with our inner child, or indeed our outer child whom we birthed.

For at the deepest level of Truth, we are all One.
One Love.
One Self.
One Being.

And we have forgotten that the disharmony we feel within our minds, is reflected out in our external lives.

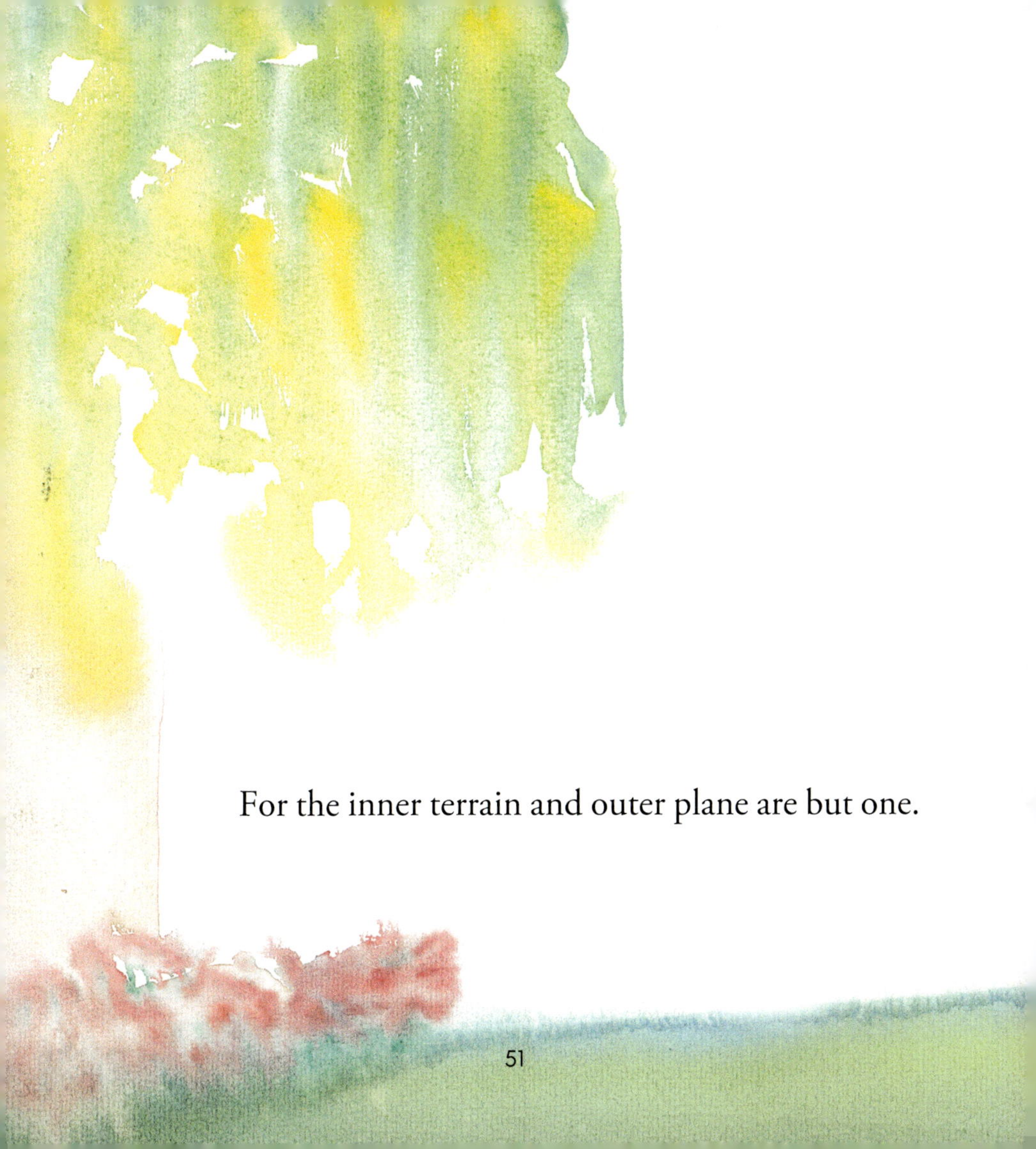

For the inner terrain and outer plane are but one.

Our hearts are in pain,
yet we have learned to
tolerate our suffering and
to parent according to
the dictates of society.

The habitual, thinking mind is **asleep**, steeped in beliefs and memories of the past it governs through guilt.
We follow rulers, religions, traditions.
We compete, comply, quantify, and qualify.

We are conditioned, trapped in roles which deplete, in jobs which no longer serve us, in minds which compute, and in hierarchies which mute.

Alas, we are starved, thirsty, fearful and guilty. And we know deep within something is desperately wrong with our world. So we seek.

And attempt to compensate with bodily pleasures.

But we are infinitely more than our bodies, our minds, and our desires, although the thinking mind tempts us to believe otherwise.

And all that glitters is merely an illusion, which offers no peace and no sustenance.

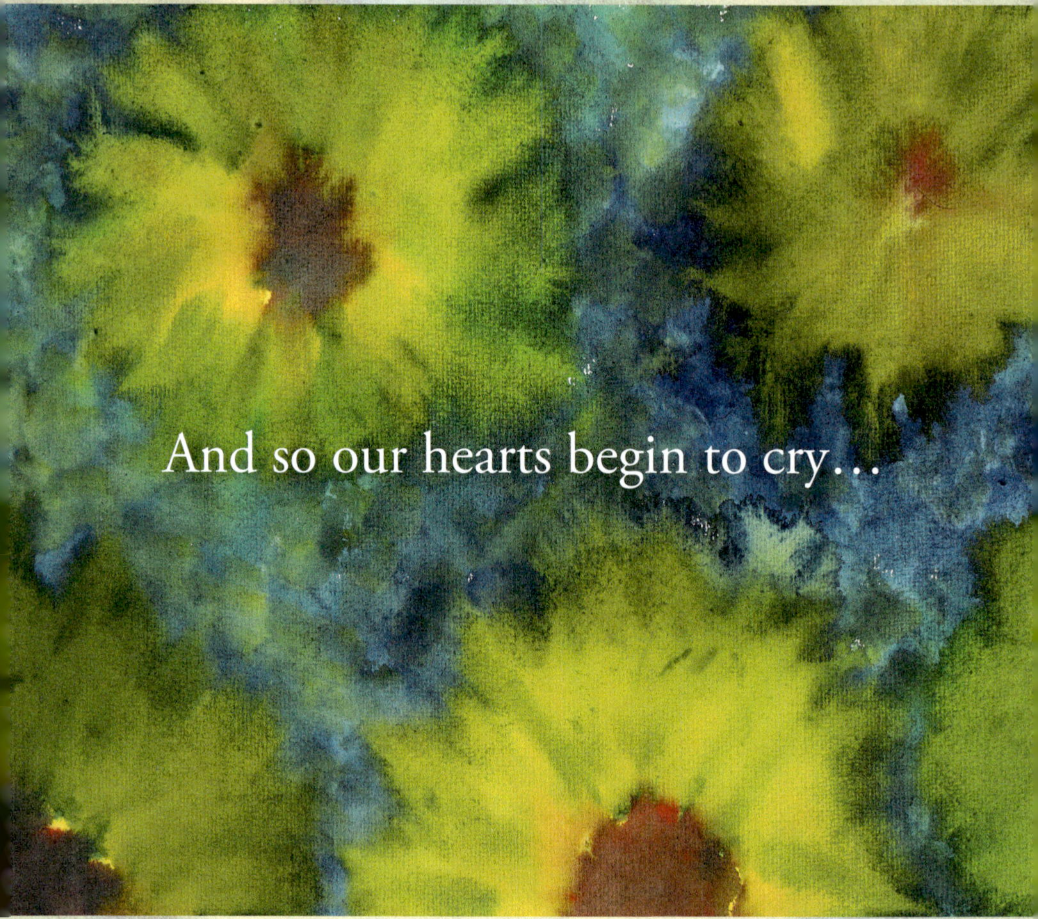

And so our hearts begin to cry…

As does our child, and we ourselves.

For the world is too loud.

We are tired, pressured by time. Overwhelmed. Exhausted.

Our child merely wishes to be seen and longs for our Love, but we do not know how to reach her.

Always resisting.

We have forgotten.

Our beautiful child dwells effortlessly within the Stillness, whilst we are attached to the chaos of our minds.

She knows of our very Presence, our Unconditional Love, and demands to be brought up in this Truth.

She longs for us to willingly join her.

This untouched Presence, so pristine, so pure, offers you a bridge from the thinking mind into Being and into Freedom.

This is your true home. The essential nature of your mind.

It is your true wealth, for your divine inheritance lies here.

It cannot be taught, bought or sold.

For it is priceless.
Innocent.
And simply Is.

Our child **seeks not** our material wealth.

But only **true union**, a bonding in friendship.

60

For this timeless space in which she sits is pure Love, Joy and Bliss.
Accept her invitation and sit down with her here, silently, and
begin to create.
Accept this moment as is.
Let her shining wisdom inform you.
Now she is your teacher.

Draw with your heart, softly, as she does, and trust the process.

Slowly, feel and sense your essence merge and expand with her
joyful Presence.

There is no right or wrong here, no judgment, no expectation, no
one to impress, no to-do list, no time, no place.

Just sacred space between mother and child.

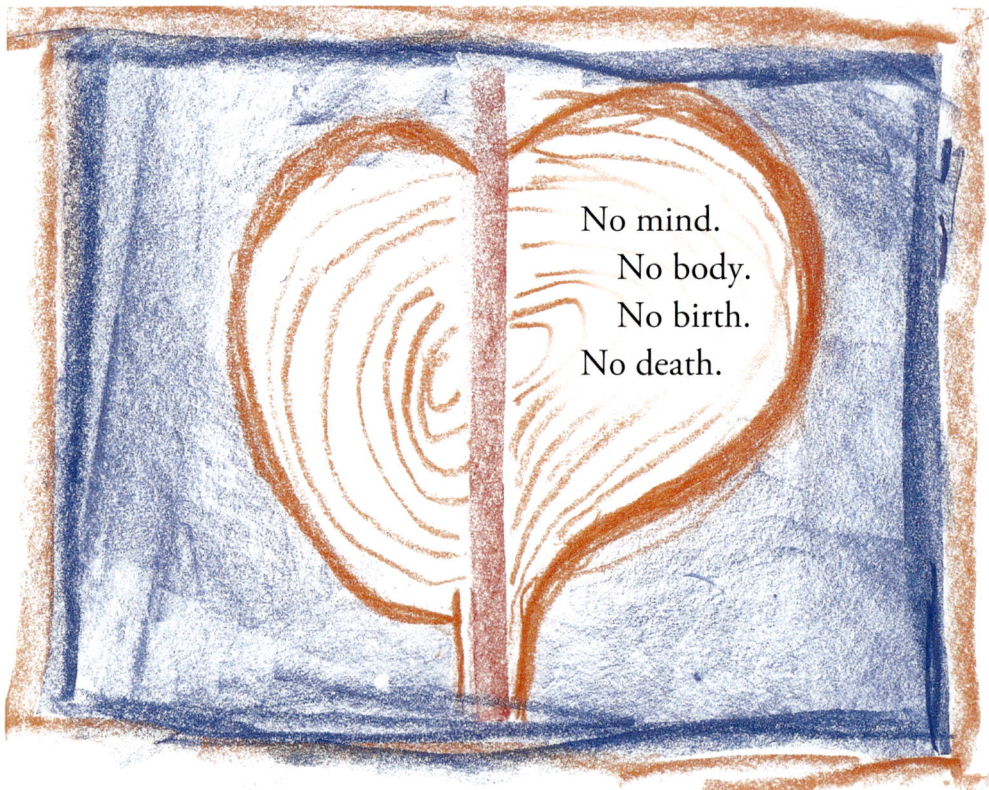

No mind.
No body.
No birth.
No death.

You draw as One BEING.
And you sit on holy ground.
Seek no more for the material world, the church, the
ashram, or the guru.
For the mountains of the Himalayas rise from within.

Only Love exists here.
And only Love is real.

The heart of your child is silently speaking, so please
mother from this Stillness.

She

radiates

a light…

64

So gentle and so bright it will begin to illuminate the darkened corners of your mind, if you are willing, and if you are open to this.

She is a messenger of peace, here to help you dissolve your internal barriers to Love's all-encompassing Presence.

Drink

from the golden nectar

which she offers,

so you may soften, deepen and begin to enquire and awaken from the dream of ancestral pain and guilt, which keeps your mind locked in repeated cycles of suffering, and robs you from experiencing each and every moment with conscious Presence.

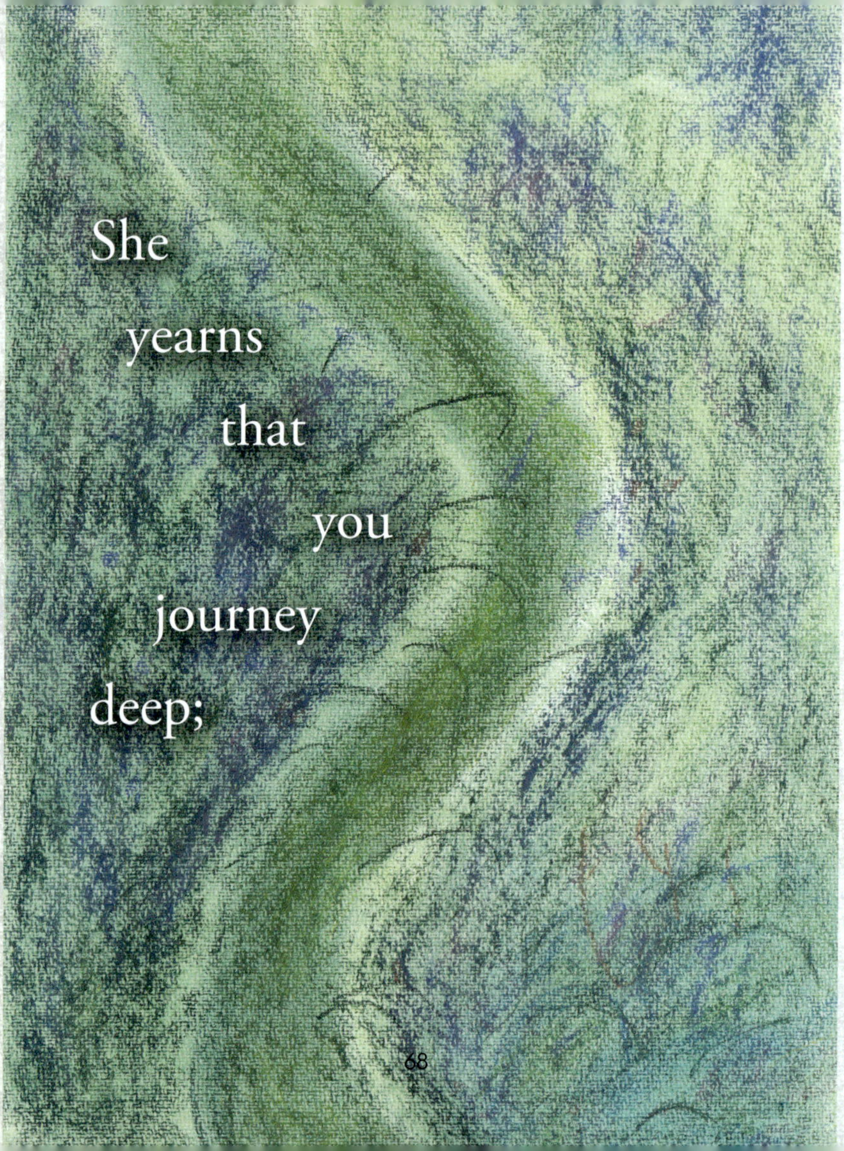

She

yearns

that

you

journey

deep;

to descend into your pain and to have the courage to embrace the weeping wounds in your heart.

Trust and be still. Be rooted.

Your heart knows what to do.

Do not run from this calling, this inner growth.

Rather find the strength to open,

one

by

one,

every door

which is a gateway to your heart.

For like Snow White, you lay asleep to your divinity.

And like the Prince, your child's Love will awaken you from the insidious dream which your thinking, judging mind has created.

For we are each painting a dream we call the world.

Your child is your soulmate and knows of your divine Source.

And at the deepest level of Truth we remember why our beloved child has come to us.

And so now we must listen.

Beloved Mother,

I ask you to **be still**, for my heart wishes to speak to you.

It is time to breathe into the tenderness of your heart.
And it is time to feel into the purity of your pain, so it
may slowly begin to dissolve.

Your darkness may scare you and anger you.
Yet I ask you to feel your anger.
Feel your pain, your disappointment, your grief.

I am innocent, simply lighting a way to Truth.
For all anger is past anger, buried anger.
And you are deeper than your anger.

Please become **aware** of your thoughts, your beliefs, your
feelings, and your bodily sensations associated with anger.
And ask, who is it that experiences this anger?

Enquire closely.

In essence, you yourself are not your thoughts, your beliefs,
your feelings, or your bodily sensations.
For like a river, they ebb and flow through you.

Please turn your gaze towards yourself, lovingly.

Rest, soften, deepen and simply ask:
What is always **awake** and **aware** as I mother?
What is it that lies behind my thoughts, feelings,
beliefs and perceptions?
Everything in my experience is continuously changing and
disappearing, yet what is it that constantly remains?

Beloved Mother,

Your darkness may upset you.
But please feel your sadness and your heartbreak, and give
yourself permission to cry.

I am innocent, simply lighting a way to Truth.
For all sadness is past sadness, buried sadness.
And you are deeper than your sadness.

Please become **aware** of your thoughts, your beliefs, your
feelings, and your bodily sensations associated with sadness.

And ask, who is it that experiences this sadness?

Enquire closely.

In essence, you yourself are not your thoughts, your beliefs,
your feelings, or your bodily sensations.
For like a river, they ebb and flow through you.

Please forgive yourself for believing in suffering,
as the ultimate Truth.

Turn your gaze towards yourself, lovingly.

Rest, soften, deepen and simply ask:
What is always **awake** and **aware** as I mother?
What is it that lies behind my thoughts, feelings,
beliefs and perceptions?
Everything in my experience is continuously changing and
disappearing, yet what is it that constantly remains?

Beloved Mother,

Your darkness may bring to the surface the tremendous
fear which resides within you.

Please have the courage to feel your fear, your anxiety,
your stress.
And recognise this suffering is a call to awaken and
connect to a deeper Self.
We chose it to be so, in this manner.

I am innocent, simply lighting a way to Truth.
For all fear is past fear, buried fear.
And you are deeper than your fear.

Please become **aware** of your thoughts, your beliefs, your
feelings, and your bodily sensations associated with fear.

And ask, who is it that experiences this fear?

Enquire closely.

In essence, you yourself are not your thoughts,
your beliefs, your feelings, or your bodily sensations.
For like a river, they ebb and flow through you.

Please turn your gaze towards yourself, lovingly.

Rest, soften, deepen and simply ask:
What is always **awake** and **aware** as I mother?
What is it that lies behind my thoughts, feelings,
beliefs and perceptions?
Everything in my experience is continuously changing and
disappearing, yet what is it that constantly remains?

Beloved Mother,

These beliefs in fear, lack and guilt, which exist within your mind, hold you back from opening into Love, into Life, into what is here Now.

These beliefs in fear, lack and guilt which exist in every human being, sit collectively, and show up as attack, disease, and war.

Please forgive me for bringing up this fear.
But I am innocent, simply lighting a way to Truth.

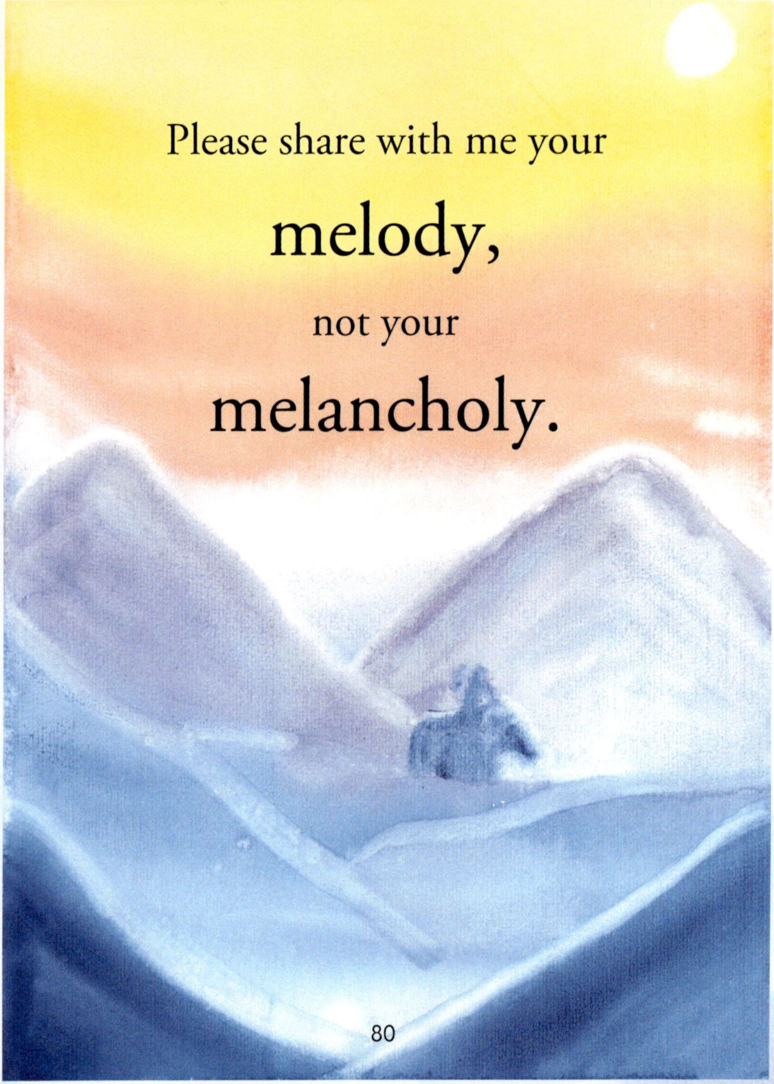

Please share with me your

melody,

not your

melancholy.

For I did not

journey here

to add burden

to your

heavy heart.

But rather to
liberate you…

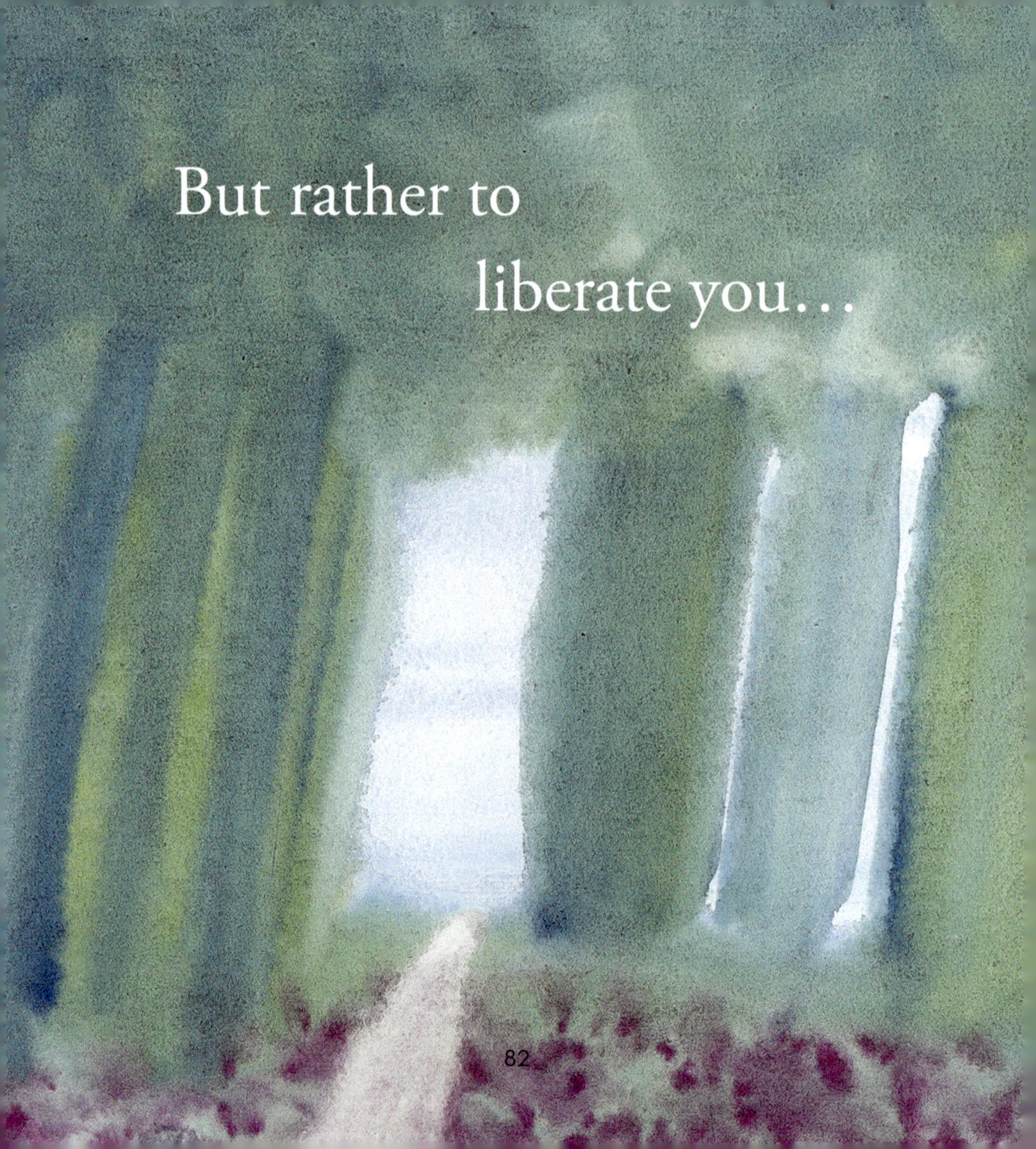

…and invite you to open your mind

to Truth.

For I Am the Flow,

as are you.

And my deepest prayer is for you to glow.

To play outside and greet the day with Love
and childlike wonder.

And
so
we
pause,
and
take
heed,

and begin together
a quest for the deepest
Truth.

Each one of us a warrior, divinely equipped for the inner journey Home.

Let us be present. Be rooted. Be still.
And welcome this moment as is.
Turning our attention inwards,
let us keep feeling.
No longer resisting.
Tenderly sensing into and through the source of our anger, pain, fear, and guilt – layer by layer – whilst being drawn gently into the loving ground of Grace within.

Only our forgiving, trusting, compassionate heart knows the way, as it guides and moves us beyond our personal history, limiting beliefs and perceptions.

And let us watch the judging mind, for it is fierce and seeks damnation.

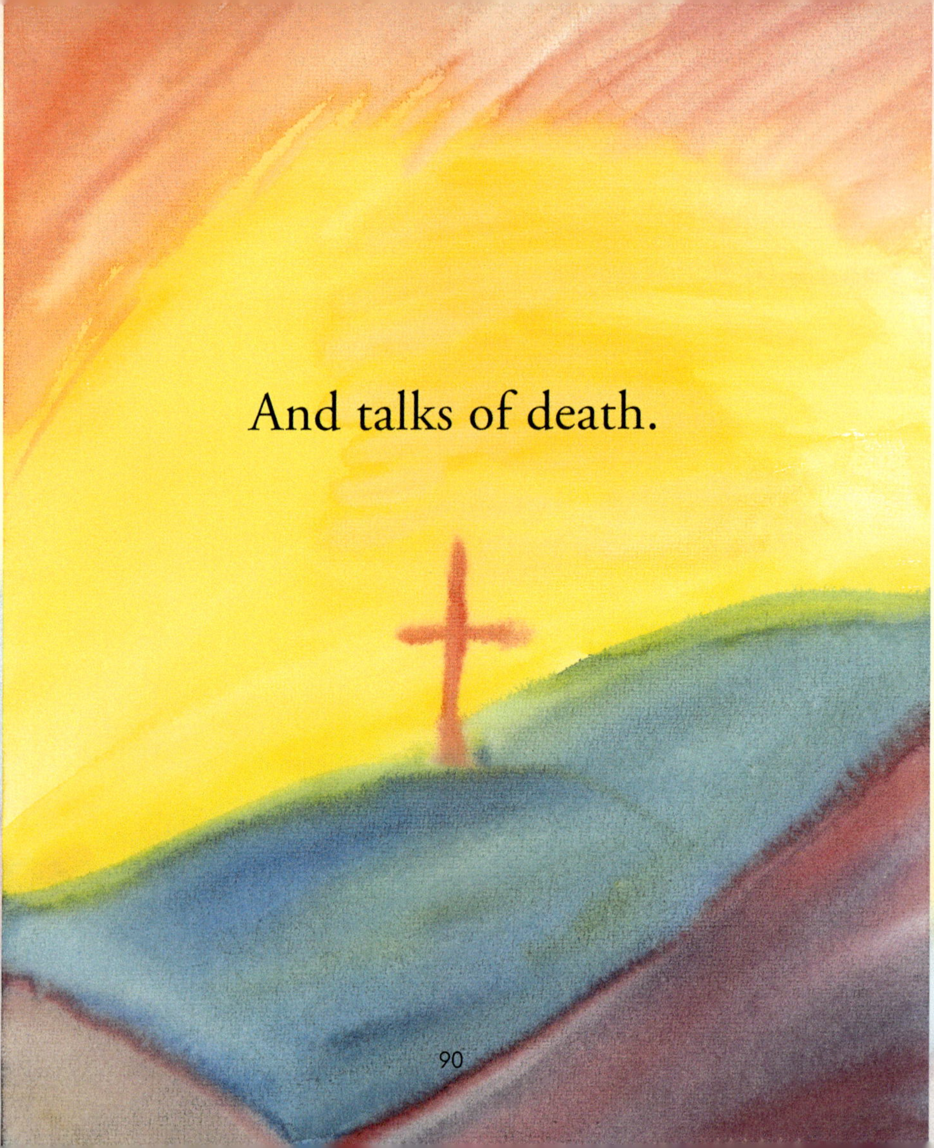

And talks of death.

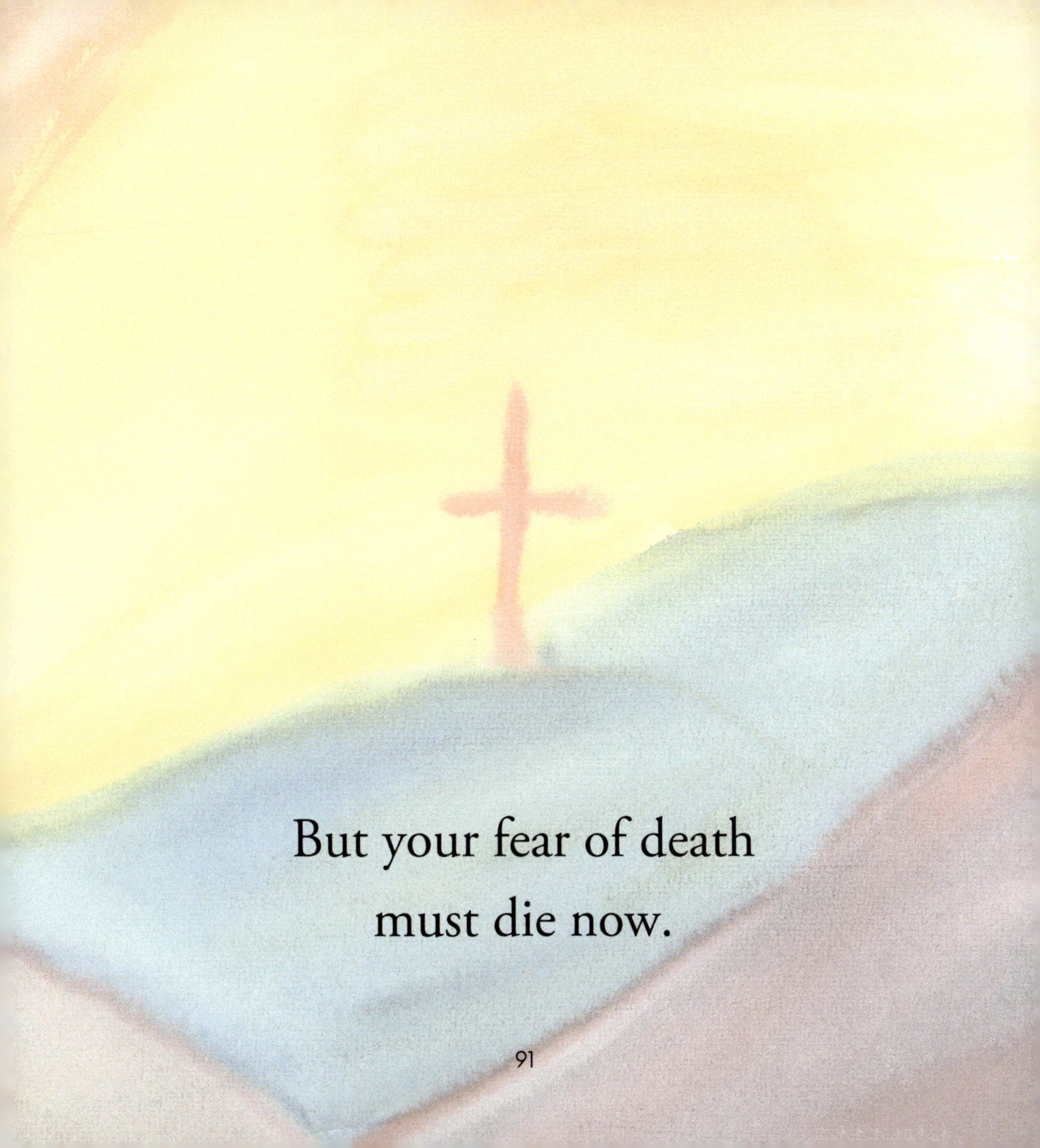

But your fear of death
must die now.

As you surrender, and merge into the ground
of Grace, and open up to the mystery,
observe as the old internal world is naturally
swept away…

Rules, **roles**, and regulations no longer serve.
You have served your time.

What is uncovered is spacious, timeless,
infinite, divine.

Silently **aware**, silently **awake**, silently **open**,
silently **abiding** within itself.

Recognised as perfection, wholeness, Love.

Rest your heart here.
As the **Love** and **Peace** that you already are.

You have always been this still, silent **awareness**,
shining as Love whilst you've mothered.

Sense yourself as

This Presence.
This Freedom.
This Stillness.

This ever-present, safe, unchanging Essence.

Know yourself as

This I Am Presence.
This I Am.
This I.

Rest Knowingly as this I and be expansive.

Feel yourself as this clear, open sky of awareness.

Witness how the play of light and dark,

naturally arises, sings, and subsides from within this Stillness.

Be the clear seeing and the silent listening, and this dream of birth and death will own you no more.

For like a river, life will dance through you.

In Truth, it never truly touched you.

Be the **aware Being**, and choose to
mother from this sacred space.

Acknowledge your darkness,
but stand firm as the Light.

And meet your child afresh, with new eyes,
ears, and an awakened heart.

Fully embodied.
As Love's Presence.

Let your Love embrace your fears,
let your Love melt your sorrows, and
let your Divine Love mother your child.

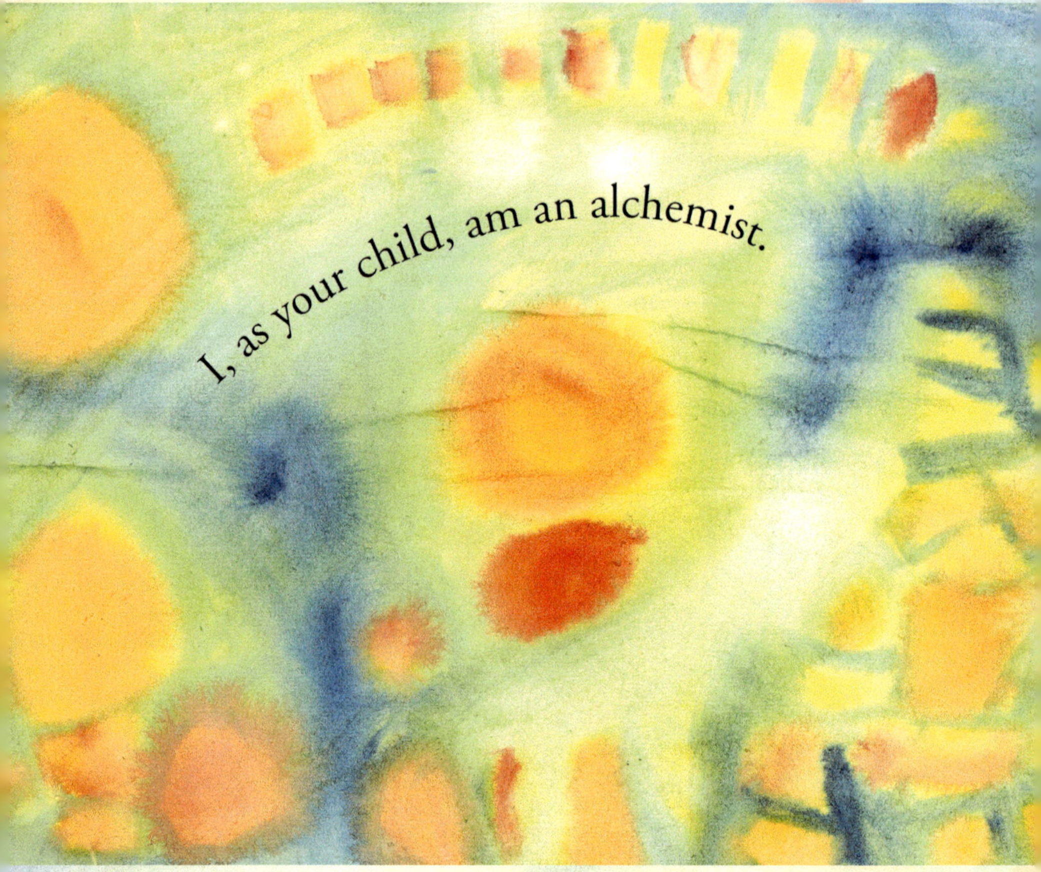

I, as your child, am an alchemist.

I hold the Truth, a bridge back home for you.

And within our voices, our laughter,
our cries and darkness,
within the heart of mothering itself,
sits a bounty of Love for you and as you,
silently awake and fully aware.

Innocent, Free, and at Peace.

My gift may seem quite ordinary.
Yet when touched by Grace,
it becomes extraordinary.

Mother, please sink into the heart of this Knowing so you may flower into your true, essential nature. No effort is needed here.

Allow this Presence to just Be.

And watch your petals open, one by one.

Please take my hand and I will guide you.

You need only find **willingness**, to begin.

Autobiography

How This Message Came To Be

I share my personal story for no other reason than to bring transparency, light, healing, and understanding into the minds and hearts of the reader. I thank my family and friends for the love and support they have bestowed in helping me to bring this message to the world.

The Story

I was born to a passionate, spiritual Indian woman who, although a Hindu, had an ardent love for Christ.

It was her pioneering heart and a desire to follow her inner counsel which lifted her out of an arranged marriage in East Africa and brought her to London in 1967 with her two young children. She had been married at the tender age of fourteen, a matrimony to which she had naively agreed in order to respect her ailing mother.

She had broken all the silent rules of an Indian woman living in a culture steeped in ancient tradition – that of respecting her parents' choice of partner, and a life purpose imbued with honouring her husband, his family, and society at large.

In London, she settled with her brother and his wife and found a part-time job. There she met my father, also a Hindu, and they came to enjoy an all-powerful love for each other. However, problems began for them when their families and the wider community found out that she was pregnant. There were also practical issues to contend with. My mother was waiting for a divorce from her former husband, with whom she already had two children, and money was tight. My father was a student who was supporting his paralysed father, his mother, and his two siblings. And now there would be three children to provide for.

It was 1970 and, at that time in Indian culture, to fall in love without the umbrella of an arranged marriage and the approval of family was simply inconceivable. In fact, to bring a child into the world out of wedlock was, in itself, deemed highly immoral. It was also a time of great repression, subjugation, emotional depression, and trauma as the Indian community and some of my parents' families were being forced to leave East Africa by the dictator, Idi Amin. Thus, their arrival on British soil was truly radical.

Whilst I was in the womb, my mother became the family scapegoat, since defying her ingrained cultural roots brought up deep feelings of resentment, anger, and unhealed collective pain. But now, close family members also began projecting their own inner fears, hidden guilt, and judgments onto her. And although she had narrowly escaped the repression in East Africa, it had followed her to England. She was ostracised by her loved ones, and began to believe she had brought immense shame onto everyone, especially as her two sisters had both married into respectable, wealthy Indian homes.

My parents were vulnerable, and began to be attacked both verbally and emotionally. My mother slowly started losing her self-worth. She lost faith in everything – herself, her own authority, God, her ability to mother, her divinity, her beauty, and her dream of freedom. Condemned for her open yet trailblazing heart, she now believed she was an embarrassment and an outlaw, and had committed a sin for simply falling in love.

Both my parents felt silenced and imprisoned.

They could, of course, have chosen a hushed-up abortion, but my mother had the will of a warrior and the vision to birth a new beginning. So, with a heart brimming with love for my father, she escaped the scathing voices of her family, took herself to a quiet village near Cheltenham in the English countryside, and gave birth to me.

And so I was brought into this world of time and space with already-indoctrinated ideas – inherited guilt, cultural conditioning, belief systems, and the lens of others through which I would perceive the world. I carried an open wound within me – the burden of ancestral karma which would hound me for years to come. This wound was an attack on the feminine in all her forms. But I too was graced with the spirit of warriorship, and inherent in my own heart was a powerful hunger for Freedom.

Within the mind and heart of every one of us sits a wound, a trauma, a guilt of this nature. It is so heavily guarded that not only do we see it repeatedly played out within ourselves and our families, but we also see it projected out within the collective human condition. This wound manifests as separation, disharmony, conflict and war.

When we identify solely with our wound, we feel alienated in this three-dimensional world of form, and believe we are limited beings trapped in separate bodies. We have no sense of the Freedom and limitlessness which is our true essential nature. We feel cut off from the infinite supply of Love, disconnected from Source, and we see no harmony or unity in life. Inevitably, this causes our most profound suffering.

A few years on, there was little peace for my mother. Her estranged husband was demanding that she return home. She had three young children to care for and there was no divorce in sight. A gossiping, threatening community left her feeling exhausted, powerless, supressed, and withdrawn, and her voice carried little weight. At the end of her tether and with an utterly broken heart, she finally saw no other option but to leave me with my grandmother and father, and she simply walked away with her two other children.

My mother's name was never again mentioned by my father during my childhood, and even as a young child I understood it was strictly forbidden to speak of her. Yet her beautiful and haunting lullabies resounded within my heart for a long, long time.

Within a couple of years my father married, and at the age of five I was taken from my grandmother and went to live with him, my stepmother, and my newborn baby sister.

Unbeknown to the family at the time, my stepmother suffered from a profound depression, which was only diagnosed years later when I was in my teens. As a consequence of her sorrow, my story can be likened to that of Cinderella. I believed I had no choice, and submitted to carrying out endless household chores on a daily basis, which deprived me of childhood play and friends. I was often beaten and my sense of self gradually diminished, as

I surrendered my individuality to attend to my family. I constantly lived in fear, walking on eggshells, and it seemed that there was no one to talk to. A part of me continually yearned for some love and approval. Sadly, there was none to be had. I grew to carry an implicit sense of responsibility for my stepmother, yet somewhere inside, I always believed I had failed her and that I was never good enough. I felt no Love and no Heart. It was as if I was in prison, in my own heart.

After much introspection and healing, I now hold the greatest compassion for my stepmother as she too, like my parents, was a first-generation Indian to grow up in East Africa. Despite having an education, a professional career, and gaining financial independence as an Asian woman in England, she also experienced disharmony within her physical, emotional, and spiritual worlds. Her innocent voice, her own dreams, and her divinity had, at some stage in her childhood, also been put soundly to sleep.

As a child, my source of love and the feeling of belonging came from the times I spent with my grandmother, a delicious, warm-hearted soul who was generous of spirit and profoundly connected with the divine. Born, raised, and educated in India, she too had been brought up by a stepmother; however, her love for the Hindu scriptures had kept her aligned in her heart. She held an open, loving space in which laughter and fun were encouraged while we sipped tea and ate "chocolate everything". Indeed, it was during these special times that I first encountered grace at play. My grandmother always made it clear that my mother had genuinely loved me, but these conversations were kept short and I never had the courage to press for more information. A loving uncle was also on the scene, but my precious visits and interactions with this beautiful soul were few and far between.

Back at home, it was in my baby sister's bedroom where I found my innermost refuge. There was an enticing red carpet and I would sit on the floor next to her cot, somehow intuitively aware of a still, palpable Presence. I was too young to understand that this very Presence was in reality my essential essence, my true nature, yet somehow, I sensed that this unmistakable awareness was cradling everything.

As a child, I was not seen for my sensitivity, depth or intuition. My essence went unnoticed, since like all the others I was ensnared in our ancestral wound. We were silenced by our own lineage, community, culture, and belief systems; all innocent, yet seemingly caught in the wheel of Samsara – the cycle of rebirth and death – governed by the laws of karma within the physical world. We each played out our roles perfectly, like puppets. And it was the super glue of guilt which kept these endless stories in place.

All the time, my father was busy trying to maintain some sense of unity in his own family, traumatised by his belief that he had somehow failed his parents. He worked very hard and later, when my stepmother was diagnosed with cancer and stopped working, he toiled most weekends.

He knew nothing of my misery, yet always implored me to maintain harmony with my stepmother. He carried the weight of the world on his shoulders, playing out the role of the Indian masculine archetype; the provider. As children we were brought up to respect and honour all elders, and my upbringing demanded that I conform. So, whilst I loved my father immensely, I was unknowingly being stifled by his fears and shortcomings.

As I grew, I understood that not only my immediate family, but also our extended family, friends, and community stayed hushed to their own hearts. Hurt and traumas were stuffed under the carpet, and that's where they stayed. Each of us followed cultural rules and traditions, meeting parents' expectations with regards to marriage. It seemed we were all lifelong prisoners in a stream of past conditioning; our beautiful, creative voices quashed and unheard.

Not one of us mentioned our inner feelings, or talked much of love. There was no space, no time. East African

Indians worked hard, in survival mode, setting up homes in a foreign country unlike their own in every respect.

And so we remained outer-focused. Money was high on the agenda as each family tried to recover from the financial losses of East Africa. At the same time, they also remained uncompromising with their children in terms of demanding high academic success. This would understandably secure good jobs for the future, yet it was a severe regime to live under.

So, with my heart securely padlocked, I too, at some stage, fell fast asleep to my true identity, my childlike wonder, and learned to reside in the conditioned, thinking mind. I actually believed I was the ego mind, the separated self, the sickness, the tragedy and the parody which plagues our planet. I felt like an outsider who was trying to fit into a family I believed I didn't belong to, into a community which had shunned me at birth, and into a primary school where I was the only Indian girl. It was never my destiny to focus on my gifts of writing, creativity, or dance, and my dreams, hopes, and visions were never discussed, for they all fell outside the norm of an acceptable, respectable career.

And so it came as no surprise when, in my early twenties, life brought me to my knees with a significant health problem. It was shortly after I graduated, when I was assigned to my first investment banking job in London. Internally I was in turmoil. An inner war was raging, and I found myself on the waiting list for a kidney transplant. It was a life-changing period in my life.

At the same time as praying for a kidney, I clearly understood that someone would have to die in order for me to survive. This felt incomprehensible, overwhelming, and left me in a state of acute self-enquiry. For months, I literally looked death in the face and found myself questioning the whole meaning of birth, life, and death. I had always hungered for a relationship with my own mother, and now I wondered if I would die without ever really knowing her. I felt unfairly treated by my mother, my father, my stepmother, by everything that had happened. I felt more than resentful – I felt deeply unloved and badly betrayed – betrayed by life itself. It was as if I hadn't ever had a chance to fully live or honestly express myself and perhaps for the first time ever, as my internal defences weakened, I allowed myself to feel the unbearable agony and utter anguish within.

I let myself weep. The feelings were excruciating, and there was no way of escaping them. I felt vulnerable, but at the same time there was an inherent sense of release, of an acceptance of my life circumstances. This illness became my teacher and I came to realise that I had repressed my authentic feelings throughout my whole life. I understood in the very depths of my being that through this emotional suppression, I had somehow unconsciously created my illness. It was in these moments of darkness that I put out a cry and a prayer for help. I called to know the Truth. I called for incisive understanding and I called for wisdom. I was desperate, but now I saw that the end of the road is always an invitation, and a doorway to liberation if we are willing to see it.

On the morning of my transplant operation, as I sat in front of my kidney consultant, something intimate yet extraordinary happened. It was subtle, but powerful. I felt an indescribable moment of infinite Love encompassing my whole being, in the same way that I had in my baby sister's bedroom. Despite my rapidly deteriorating body, a sense of vitality arose within me. It was an all-encompassing state of acceptance and peace which totally filled my heart and held me like a child. I sensed the Divine Mother. Initially there was a feeling of relief, as it seemed that through my senses, my attention was gently being drawn inwardly back home to Source, and into the loving depths and ground of Grace within. There was a sense of quiet joy and wellbeing even. In this space, it was almost inconceivable to believe that I was really ill, and in need of a life-saving transplant.

I tried to dismiss this experience, putting it down to high

toxicity levels and an unclear mind, but as I began to rest in and as this expansive field of Presence, I was momentarily lifted out of the content of my mind, and began to subtly sense my essential nature. I found myself sitting for a whole ten hours, unable to actually say Yes (or give the final go ahead) to my imminent transplant surgery. I sat without worry, absorbed in a timeless Stillness, an infinite Truth deeper than my intellect, and leaving my surgeon confused as to why I was questioning this new gift of life.

As I began to look upon my human story through the eyes of compassion, it became clear that if I were to accept this kidney from a recently deceased donor, then attached to it was a profound, karmic responsibility. I understood that in order to honour this sacred gift, a realignment of my life would have to be called forth. It was apparent that I was identified entirely with my fearful, protective, separate self. I was rooted in guilt and fear and had unconsciously created an inner terrain of polluted waters within my body, which were now in need of a deep cleanse. I was being asked to meet with my life fully, to enquire into and attend to my inner sorrow with integrity and tenderness, for my childhood wounds were each simply asking to reveal their own history, story, emotion, and deeper truth.

Only through contemplation and sincere curiosity would I eventually be able to forgive my resentments, and let go of my perceived fears whilst staying open to this intimate Loving Presence – thus cleansing my inner waters and giving my new kidney a chance to survive.

I sensed my path would unfold one step at a time, and subsequently I came to understand this all-encompassing, Self abiding field as the Loving Presence of awareness, the Knowing of my Being – my deeper Self, my true Self.

Two years later, and after a successful kidney transplant, I was touched by this beautiful Presence once again when my son, Jamie, was born. One look into his baby eyes and I was instantly connected, and held in a beautiful, warm space of Love. It was a moment in which thought disappeared, including all memory of the pain of labour and birth. Only Love was present, and whilst transient, it was totally palpable.

As I began to mother, I was confronted with aspects of my mind that begged to be healed, forgiven, and returned to wholeness. It was not easy, as these unhealed parts insisted that I was not cut out to be a mother. They kept whispering that I couldn't be present with my child, that I was not liberated or free to express myself, to play or have fun. Since I was still so desensitised by my early conditioning, I actually believed these untruths and remained shut down, feeling contracted and burdened. I was faced with a terrified part of myself which tempted me to run from mothering, insidiously reminding me that I was not good enough to fulfil this beautiful calling. The ego mind lured me to keep seeking in the outer world for the Love I desperately believed I lacked, when all the time my glorious child was reminding me of my essential nature, awake within everything.

I sought professional support to help heal from my childhood trauma, gradually attuning and aligning with my heart, body and mind. And as I began to make substantial headway on my healing journey, I was brought to the spiritual and psychological teachings of *A Course in Miracles*, via my young son's wonderful nursery group in 2002. *The Course*, as it is known, is an in-depth study of Christ Consciousness, and the teachings of forgiveness contained within its workbook pages became my daily prayer and practice.

It was at this time that my mother also came back into my life. Her own internal pain had carried her through church doors, and she had undergone a personal rebirth of energy, becoming a missionary who travelled the world and taught the Bible. I was aware of my suppressed rage towards her, my hurt, my feelings of abandonment, shame, heartbreak, and judgments, and I acknowledged my desire to attack and blame her. However, as I deepened into *The Course,* I also understood that if I stayed in judgment of my mother then I was choosing to judge and attack myself, for she was showing me the hidden perceptions of guilt and lovelessness, I too had come here to heal. But this went even deeper. It was also about my son, and in order for me to parent without bias, and open my mind and my heart, I had to confront my shadows and take responsibility for my own feelings, thought systems, coping mechanisms, and unhealthy, limiting core beliefs.

At the most refined level of Truth, I began to understand we are but one Love and one Mind, only ever meeting ourselves in any interaction.

Within my physical body was a young, transplanted kidney, a gift from the divine, and to give this kidney a chance to survive, to thrive even, I realised it was now time to clean up the unhealed beliefs and perceptions associated with all my relationships.

My early years of mothering thus became a time of great compassion and humility, and a time for uncompromising honesty. With grace, guidance, and support, I started to venture down into the shadowy recesses of my mind in order to shine a light on the darkness, the fear, the pain, the anger, and the resentment, which had been lurking there for years. I understood that only by exploring it all, and feeling through the suppressed sensations and emotions held within my body, would I eventually begin to move beyond these murky bogs, and start to receive Love from my son, my mother, and my family – the Love I had rejected and denied, perhaps for lifetimes. I became hugely grateful for the roles each person was playing. They had all agreed, energetically, to dance with me in this incarnation, offering an opportunity to help heal the collective unconscious mind as well as our ancestral line, thus touching the higher Love that sits beyond personality.

I began to recognise that my suffering world was my creation, a projection of the unloving thoughts, beliefs and unconscious guilt which I had taken on at birth and absorbed as a young child. A mirror of my mind. I realised it really was all a dark yet holographic representation of my most unhealed values. I was tired of running, exhausted by constantly attempting to keep my hurt at bay, unintentionally projecting guilt onto others, blaming and shaming. Even my transcendental meditation practice had become an attempt to bypass my feelings of failure, unworthiness, self-loathing, and the grief associated with my own perceived tragedy. More than ever, I understood it was time to take responsibility for my projections and to meet every illusion with honesty, for these stories had run their course and I had no wish for my son to inherit them. It was time to actualise my life, going deeper into my childhood pain and calling forth a power beyond my own to restore innocence, wholeness and unity.

My young son of course offered me Unconditional Love, and the trust needed for me to walk a path of forgiveness, surrendering into the unknown and gradually letting go of my belief in separation. Without being aware of what he was doing, he held me in Love and in Truth, and brought so much to light. And as my commitment to heal grew, I was met and trained with a beautiful circle of teachers who each illuminated my path and pointed me back to the transformational journey of self-forgiveness.

True forgiveness cannot take place in the mind, as it is not a meagre apology. Instead it allows a metamorphosis to occur in the heart, when the mind is open to healing.

It is primarily a call to Peace and Truth, and then it becomes a meeting with our own thoughts, beliefs, fears, pain, and guilt, and a rendezvous with our heartache, hatred, and judgments. Ultimately, it becomes a choice to completely transcend our grievances, whilst being held in the depths of Love and an acceptance of all that is. It is a complete letting go of all control, judgments, stories, and definitions; and a yielding into the arms of grace. It is where humanity meets with divinity, and it is here that we complete our process as we totally surrender our minds into Love and allow the aliveness of Presence to arise — accepting the gift to thrive and to live, to dance and to breathe this extraordinary mystery we call Life.

It is an atonement, an acknowledgement of our essence, thus allowing true perception to be restored.

I understood it was time for me to mother from a place of real devotion. To welcome and forgive my grievances, and to join and courageously accept every aspect of my son, this divine Being, seeing him anew and with innocence and clarity, dispelling untruths and meeting him beyond the veils of *Maya* and the illusion of my ego mind.

When my daughter, Sienna, entered the world some six years later, an even deeper surrender was called forth. During her birth, a primordial chant from a wellspring within expressed itself through me, however I was not the one who was doing the chanting. Yes, a sacred chant was emanating, but I was being chanted. And so, arrival was honoured with song as we both birthed into the world. It was indescribably beautiful and beyond words.

Her birth summoned me to move past the conditioned mind. With ease, I gave myself up to the divine within and experienced a changeless, timeless Love, which allowed me to respond to my child intuitively and effortlessly both in the middle of the night and at the breaking of dawn. I finally knew this Love as the ground of ultimate Truth.

Sienna's presence brought a luxurious Stillness into the home, leading me ultimately to the teacher within. In search of the origins of my mystical chant, I was led into the awakened Presence and beautiful teachings of Chloë Goodchild, Eckhart Tolle and Rupert Spira, who in turn led me to the teachings of the great saints of India, namely Anandamayi Ma – The Bliss Permeated Mother – and Sri Ramana Maharshi.

Chloë's teachings allowed me to enter into the mystical practice of mantra and sound meditation and I began to reclaim my innate, naked voice, which had been silenced as a child. Through mantra and a gentle inner-enquiry into my pain, my heart tenderly opened, and I found myself naturally surrendering into the Presence of the Divine Mother within. She was so vast and blissful. I felt her compassion, and her grace and calm as I chanted through my childhood sorrow, and I recognised our One unified voice as the sacred Loving field, which had been palpable at Sienna's birth.

I understood my children were asking that the qualities of this deeper Love be shared with them, and Jamie's and Sienna's births had both delivered an undeniably clear instruction to me. I had been starved of this precious, nourishing energy as a child, and for my children to truly blossom and prosper, I realised my path was not negotiable. Their hearts were asking for a childhood founded in creativity, balance, beauty, rhythm, authority of self and the honouring of their true divine nature. In turn, I understood that as their mother, I would be called to stay fully conscious and always present in my heart and body mind.

I took to contemplating and meditating daily, silently,

becoming more present, and awake to my eternal essence. And as life gently unfolded I began to witness the unfettered Love which poured through my daughter's Being, I was able to open more profoundly, and extend my heart naturally towards the feminine, my stepmother, my mother, and those around me. A genuine healing had taken place.

In the last few months of my mother's life, I experienced without question the Love that permeates everything. Together we felt replenished, fed, acknowledged, and nurtured as we honoured each other's journey. We both reclaimed our hearts. We had each been seen, heard, and cherished, and at last I felt undeniably loved. In this sweet space, I completely understood that there never had been anything to forgive, since beyond all the drama, the stories and the illusion of my ego mind, a loving awareness had quietly encompassed us both. We were but one, one Love, one Being, experiencing an emptiness yet a magnificent and unbounded wholeness. In this vortex of eternal Love there was no birth or death, no bodies, no separation; just pure tranquility. Here, for days, we sat in sacred silence and communicated without words.

"The holiest of all spots on earth is where an ancient hatred has become a present love." [1]

At the time of her death, my family also joined in unity – my father, stepmother, sisters, brother, husband, and extended family – all brought together in the unshakeable ground of uncompromising Truth. A Love beyond personality and differences was felt by us all and we experienced without question that only Love is real. My own story of abandonment, separation and feeling unloved quickly began to fade, since we had somehow all been liberated when we chose to shake hands with the Truth. It was clear that fear had bound me to the world, and forgiveness had set me free. In Knowing my mother's innocence, I had

1   *A Course in Miracles. Chapter 26: The Transition. IX. For they have come. Published in 1976 by the Foundation for Inner Peace.*

felt my own. In years to come I was to realise my mother had granted me the Freedom to simply Be.

Her death heralded an exquisite end of the once-upon-a-time nightmare. An end of material seeking. An end of spiritual seeking via teachers, books, and workshops. An end even of a twenty-year relationship with my husband, for I understood he no longer recognised me. Yet held in infinite Love there was a perfection and acceptance of everything. It felt as if my whole world had dropped away and I was being called to move further into the depths of my own heart.

To know the Truth and experience a state of immutable Being is one thing, but to experience and walk this unfolding mystery in every waking moment, with two young children by my side, was quite another. I was unable to do it alone, so I placed my very life into the hands of the divine and surrendered myself into the unknown, trusting that my pathway would be revealed, one step at a time. And it was.

My daughter's pure, sensitive nature called forth a

conscious education at the very time when my son's heart was also asking to be tenderly nourished, for his private schooling was training his mind only to pass exams. This conscious education, which nurtured Beingness and offered a unique path to Freedom and an alignment with Truth and Integrity, opened up in the form of a Waldorf Steiner school. With no further thought, I moved with my two children to Hertfordshire and a loving community welcomed us. Stillness became my teacher. Stillness, and my two children.

A simple, slow life unfurled over the next nine years, allowing a process of integration to take place. I began to digest all that I had journeyed through and experienced. An expansion of consciousness took place in my kitchen as I cleaned, cooked, played, and rested with my children. And there was not one Himalayan mountain in sight. My Hindu origins offered beautiful mantras which cocooned and aligned the three of us as I processed my days with adoration.

More layers of the ego mind, filled with temptations of every kind, came up to be examined, explored viscerally, and forgiven. Fear, doubt, attack, guilt, and anger all knocked on my door and I welcomed them.

I began to reflect on Papaji's teachings, understanding that when we seek the Truth, every force in the universe conspires to work for our highest good, and all the Gods and Demons, wishing to reclaim us, pay a visit.

For a while, lawyers and courtrooms dominated as my divorce was finalised, forcing me to look again at the deception and contrivances of the conditioned ego thought system. I discovered that dormant anger, judgments, and projections were all still alive. Again and again, I went into forgiveness, dedicating myself to clarity and inner wisdom. I welcomed it all, and as I enquired further into the root of my suffering, and embraced my pain with complete openness, and without resistance I naturally began to ground, day by day, as the unchanging Stillness. I gently softened as my heart opened and deepened, and I did not run from my despair, for I knew unequivocally that my serenity lay in the heart of experience. I gave myself permission to simply Be, allowing myself to cry rivers of healing tears, lovingly feeling and sensing through my feelings, whilst being drawn ever deeper into the subtle, compassionate ground of Grace within. It was a natural surrender; a profound letting go of my fears and beliefs in separation, and a direct path to my deeper Self – my true Self – laid with a new foundation. I understood with conviction that the world was here only to wake me up.

As the years went by, my attachments to my unloving thoughts and judgments no longer enticed or consumed me, and no longer held the power to tempt me into purposeless action, or the expenditure of energy in the outside world. I had quietly matured.

A Course in Miracles teaches us that temptations are but attempts to make illusion real, and as I met the challenges of life with certainty and trust, this growing awareness gave me the courage to notice my thoughts with gentleness and without self-attack. Thus, the nuances and disguised masks of ego untruths just dropped away.

All through this, the children kept me grounded, aligned, and rooted. I derived tremendous pleasure from being with Mother Earth and spent time quietly contemplating in nature, listening to the birds sing and watching the clouds glide by and so too my thoughts. And this led me to open naturally into the realms of the compassionate human heart.

Slowly, I was also drawn back into the arms of my grandmother. Her overflowing love had now spilled out into the Hindu, Gujarati community and she was offering *satsang* in West London twice a week, a sacred space for 200 women to join with each other. In losing her son, my uncle, she understood the necessity of bringing healing into the heart of the Indian East African community. She was now in her eighties and provided a safe environment in which elderly women could grieve, play, pray, dance, cook, and eat. Grandmothers who were living a life of solitude and desperation in their own homes were once again embracing life, joined in purpose. They were reclaiming their voices, their femininity, and their hearts as they passionately sang mantras and bhajans, performed pujas, and artis; colourful rituals for peace and in celebration to the Gods. Diwali, Christmas, and Full Moon ceremonies were all enjoyed.

I honestly felt I had been birthed to witness the perfect nature and generosity of this darling soul. I felt her *dharshan*, her blessing, which quietly emanated from her humble Presence and was now being extended into the community at large. She was a living beauty and her life was one of pure service and Unconditional Love.

Back at home, I began to connect, meet, and see my children with even more clarity, and started to live consciously from a place of grace, play, and a quiet joy. They introduced colour, vibrancy, laughter, and a freshness into my daily life, and in turn I honoured their uniqueness, their intelligence, their gifts, their voices, and their love of painting and creativity. As a result, I welcomed my own creativity, my words, and my healing gifts; qualities inherent in the fullness of Being which slowly restored sacredness to mothering.

The seeing that emerged was not through my conditioned mind and physical eyes, but through the transparency of pure awareness, pure Being. A simple yet tangible shift in attention had taken place internally, and I was no longer looking for love, but simply receiving the world as Love; as a treasured jewel.

Through this unconditioned deeper lens, I watched in awe as my children thrived, grew, laughed, cried, picked daisies, and cycled. Everything I had been searching for was right there, in front of my very eyes. In Truth, I was all of it and there was an overflowing richness, a timeless, calm awareness, which was present in my heart; I abided there. I was the Source itself. I was overcome by peace, a sense of fulfilment, and saw that my children were offering me treasures through their essence – their simple gestures, their majesty, their aliveness, and their spontaneity. Resting Knowingly as awareness, as Stillness, as this deeper ground, I embraced a world of interconnectedness which can so easily be missed by busy parents moving in a mesmerising, transitory world; seeking for love and happiness through material possessions, imagined futures, and special relationships – where we look to another to fulfil our own perceived sense of lack.

I now understand that until we stop betraying ourselves, we can never fully experience lasting inner peace or happiness. It cannot be found in the world of form, through others, or through material wealth, and can only be experienced as we deepen and truly come to realise our true essential, ever-present nature.

It had become clear to me that the external world (the out-picturing of our minds) is here only to help us to become conscious, and so that peace and joy can be fully unveiled. As we rest Knowingly in and as awareness, where the thinking mind no longer owns us or tempts us into suffering, we are invited into timelessness and Freedom. Here, alive intelligence and clarity abides, and so we naturally choose peace and extend peace. And arising from this Knowing space is our authentic expression, creativity, and natural beauty; a fluid dance and the purity of purpose.

I once owned a magnificent home with a swimming pool. I owned a Porsche. I lived in Chelsea and my son was privately schooled in Belgravia. It seemed that I had it all, yet nothing came even close to the passion and quiet joy which I had now started to experience in my life on a daily basis.

Slowly, I began to walk with an enormous sense of gratitude in every step. I listened to my children's worries and dreams, guiding them through rites of passage and helping them to stay connected to their feelings and their hearts, so as to establish confidence within themselves. It was not all plain sailing, but as I watched without judgment from a deeper ground and allowed every situation to develop of its own accord, I found perfection within imperfection. And there was no more struggle or fear; just full acceptance.

At times, my children and I communicated without words, just as I had done with my mother. It was intensely sustaining to us all. It became clear to me that when a child's essential nature is recognised and mirrored back to them through Stillness, they remain closer to their authentic Being. A wholesomeness is present: they have a sense of self-worth, an inner confidence shines forth and empathy and compassion blossom in their hearts.

Within this safe and trusting heart space, mothering was naturally happening through me. The pain-filled, heavy thoughts and conditioned karmic patterns had been lifted and Life was revealing itself, moment by moment. I experienced a flow, and I understood that we were the flow; we were not three but one. I had experienced a total shift in my perception and the realisation that at this level of Truth, everything in this space-time continuum is an expression of Grace herself. I comprehended that all past pain is Love begging to be seen and acknowledged, and once we are willing to go directly into our suffering, we find a gateway into Life itself. My limiting beliefs and my capacity to love were all that had ever been in question, and now it seemed that life was merely arising out of Love, ebbing and flowing like waves on an ocean in an endless, fluid dance.

I knew, undoubtedly, I had never merely been a separated self, with a wound or a story. These were only ideas of the ego mind, a false identity, which had been brought to the light to be dissolved. An experience of form, arising within the formless; a paradox.

My essential nature had simply been overlooked, for it is not of this world. It has no form, and thus it cannot be seen, touched or owned, yet it has always been resting here as my deepest Self. Indeed my life and world had danced within it, as it. Silently awake at the age of five. Palpable on the morning of my transplant operation. Effortlessly present Now – transparent, eternal, timeless, ageless, invulnerable, pristine, undiminished, unspeakable even. Constantly aware of itself, sitting quietly in the background, whilst the loud story of "me" played out in the foreground. Like a blank canvas on which my colourful, creative life had been ever-unfolding, this awareness was holding the play of light and dark in the palm of her hand, like the Divine Mother.

It is this awareness which is lovingly present as we take our first breath, and present as we take our last, as we give up our worldly body. As I watched my grandmother's coffin enter the fire at her cremation, my sense of separation momentarily dissolved, as I felt her all-encompassing, loving Presence merge with my essence. And I realised that it is this shining essence that animates our short life here; giving it form and vibrancy, allowing this play of life and death to take place.

All is Known and comes into Being out of this conscious awareness, this aliveness, this Love, which is who we truly are.

With this clarity, I was able to step back and see the total perfection of my family of origin, my children, and all of life. I could welcome the majesty of utter, magnificent ordinariness.

I was reminded of a time when my daughter was in womb. As I looked out upon the sea that day, I merged with the scenery and became the sky, the ocean, the clouds. I was all of it, and I was within everything. Inner and outer were one and I was conscious only of Source, of an absolute, pristine Universal Love.

There is no telling when it is time for each of us to awaken from the ego's dream of separation, for only the divine holds this plan and only our precious heart can help bring it to fruition. There is no strategy and no methodology, since the nature of awakening is beyond the thinking mind. However, we are always gifted an open invitation from

Spirit and asked to question our perceived identity, so we may discover fully our True Reality.

The Curriculum is simple. Moment by moment, we are given the opportunity to intelligently enquire, explore, and open into our direct experience of suffering – meeting it exactly as it is, with trust, tenderness and understanding, and to resist our feelings no more, for our capacity to forgive and to Love is boundless. Love is the only healer and as we consciously welcome our pain, piece by piece, we literally "love it to death". This death then serves as a gateway, a natural surrender into the silent, ground of Being, which is our true essential nature.

The ego mind fears this death, but also fears Love – and so is always tempting us to control our inner experience, to cling to the past, and to remain in repeated and reactive cycles of emotional and mental suffering. Yet as we stay connected and keep surrendering into the Stillness within, this new ground of Grace becomes our stable foundation, and the transitory world of form fades into the background. Now, a deeper intelligence begins to work through us, and we are no longer identified with the conditioned mind and separated self but are instead the witnessing Presence. And thus, we become aware of the thoughts, images, beliefs, and stories which run through our minds and are able to merely observe them and the roles we play, rather than becoming enmeshed, and identified with them. And as we keep deepening and examining into the essential nature of our mind, we realise that all thoughts, feelings, perceptions, and sensations, are fleeting, and we are indeed the unchanging Stillness, the aware "*I Am*" Presence, in which all experience and existence arises.

Resting Knowingly as this Presence, we can now drop the label 'suffering' from our mind and experience our pain as merely a feeling, a sensation, a raw pulsating energy. And as we compassionately welcome this energy within the all-accepting field of Presence that we are, we can simply feel it through to its core, without the need to change or fix it, and allow it to run its course. In this way, the energy behind the feeling and negative emotion is neutralised, and our painful thoughts, beliefs, unconscious guilt, and memories attached to our suffering, naturally loosen their grip. And little by little, from the inside out, the ego identity starts to melt away. That which no longer serves us recedes, and the depths of Freedom and the Loving Presence of awareness remain. Indeed, this pure awareness is alive, real, and shining within the heart of all experience, and as we rest in and as this Knowing, we begin to live life as our true Self, with an authentic sense of clarity, trust, peace, quiet joy, and renewed vitality.

The appearance of the world doesn't change, and our daily lives continue to unfold with all their challenges. However, as we keep welcoming our suffering into the Stillness, our interpretation and perception of the world slowly shifts as we find no contradiction within. We no longer see the past projected outwards but rather find ourselves meeting our world through the deeper lens of Reality. Thus, our world is reflected back to us as alive, fresh, and rediscovered and we begin to experience the connectedness - the essence and beauty of all things and beings emanating from the One Source. It is then that we truly realise that beyond gender, colour and race lies only One Love, one consciousness.

During childhood, we innocently moved away from the sanctuary within our hearts. We lost connection with our inner Stillness, this ground of Grace, and feeling unloved, separate, and guilty, went searching for it in the world. However, we come to realise that we are already everything we have constantly looked for and believed we had lacked, and it is this internal shift in consciousness we are each being called to embrace. It is an invitation to keep feeling through our wounding, our deepest suffering, whilst bringing a more profound dimension of embodied Presence, honesty, and authenticity into our daily lives.

It seems Humanity is going through a transfiguration process, a global shift, and every life experience has but one request – that we stand firm as the expansive Light of awareness, and face both our personal and collective 'dark night of the soul'. It is time to recognise that our wound is a sacred gift, a critical gateway which has the potential to lead each one of us to higher wisdom, and a deeper life purpose and destiny.

In Truth, there have never been any mistakes, as our unique path is always lit, and we are being benevolently guided in every moment. We need struggle no more. The call is simply for us to be willing to keep diving deeper within, into the unknown, so we may meet each day as innocent and curious children. And in opening into this Presence, the conditioned mind gradually surrenders and is integrated back into the depths of its Source. And only then can wisdom begin to softly reveal herself and guide us through the silence of our awakened heart.

It was Jesus who said, "Truly I tell you, unless you change and become like little children, you will never enter the kingdom of Heaven".

So, when gazing into the eyes of your children, go beyond all your expectations, hopes, judgments, fears, and guilt, and greet them from the very depths of your Being. Resting there, you will both feel cherished, honoured, and whole. In this allowing, open space, nothing more will need to be said, and your work as a mother will be impeccably complete. And the Mystery which abides in your heart will dance passionately with you and as you; healing and gently lifting the hearts within your homes, your families, your communities, and humanity at large.